ROMANCE IN THE AIR

A WORLD OF ADVENTURE FOR

CORE SYSTEM

WRITING & ADVENTURE DESIGN
BILL WHITE

DEVELOPMENT
**ROB DONOGHUE &
CLARK VALENTINE**

EDITING
JOSHUA YEARSLEY

ART DIRECTION
JESSICA BANKS

LAYOUT
FRED HICKS

INTERIOR & COVER ARTWORK
DIEGO RODRIGUEZ

CARTOGRAPHY
PRISCILLA SPENCER

PROJECT MANAGEMENT
SEAN NITTNER

MARKETING
CARRIE HARRIS

BUSINESS DEVELOPMENT
CHRIS HANRAHAN

EVIL HAT
PRODUCTIONS

D0986386

An Evil Hat Productions Publication
www.evilhat.com • feedback@evilhat.com
@EvilHatOfficial on Twitter
facebook.com/EvilHatProductions

Romance in the Air
EHP0010 • Softcover ISBN 978-1-61317-097-7
Copyright © 2014 Evil Hat Productions, LLC and Bill White.
All rights reserved.

First published in 2014 by Evil Hat Productions, LLC.
10125 Colesville Rd #318, Silver Spring, MD 20901.

Evil Hat Productions and the Evil Hat and Fate logos are
trademarks owned by Evil Hat Productions, LLC. All rights reserved.

No part of this publication may be reproduced, stored in a
retrieval system, or transmitted in any form or by any means,
electronic, mechanical, photocopying, recording, or otherwise,
without the prior express permission of the publisher.

That said, if you're doing it for personal use, knock yourself out.
That's not only allowed, we encourage you to do it.

For those working at a copy shop and not at all sure if this means
the person standing at your counter can make copies of this thing, they can.
This is "express permission." Carry on.

This is a game where people make up stories about wonderful, terrible,
impossible, glorious things. All the characters and events portrayed in this
work are fictional. Any resemblance to real people, soldiers with ridiculous
accents, doughty heroes and heroines with stiff upper lips, alternate
histories both known and unknown, blushing sky-captains, or frankly the
entire steampunk genre, is purely coincidental, but kinda hilarious.

CONTENTS

Oh, those golden, heady, glorious days before the War! Those dashing young sky-hussars in their smart uniforms! Those gallant young men with their silk scarves and flying togs, escorting the pert and gaily frivolous red-cheeked daughters of the gentry! The energetic buzzing of their aerial machines as they flitted hither and yon, to alight upon the decks of balloon-hostel and cloud-salon—the oh-so-fashionable meeting places of the well-to-do, high above the petty concerns of the earthbound hoi polloi. *Off we'd go, giddy with excitement, to aerial balls and sky-borne cotillions, while below us the peaceful and well-ordered landscape floated past! Little then did we realize how fragile was our little world, how precariously we were perched in the skies above, and how little it would take to bring us all crashing down…*

In *Romance in the Air*, you'll play men and women caught up in a whirl of romance and intrigue in a *fin de siècle* Europe that never was, while around them—driven by the secret machinations of ambitious men—their civilization spirals toward a cataclysmic outbreak of war and revolution!

Our ambition is to meld the romance and drama of 19th century British drawing room fiction (all very pensive and mannered) with the freewheeling flamboyance of the pulp tradition that is the hallmark of Fate gaming. If the effect is redolent of that which has come to be called *steampunk*, we can be in no wise to blame. In fact, we unabashedly embrace the accusation. Let it be so! Austen with airships! Dickensian dirigibles! Technocratic Trollope! It is a consummation devoutly to be wished!

WHAT GENRE IS THIS, ANYWAY?

So what kind of game is it? Steampunk pulp romance with a side order of political intrigue? Yes. *Final Fantasy*-inflected alternate history cum relationship drama? Yes. *The Last Exile* meets *Downton Abbey* with a dollop of *Dr. Zhivago*? Yes, yes, yes. The real question is, what are the fictional touchstones that you—and the people with whom you're playing—want bring to the table?

It's worth it to go back to the source. You might read some Jane Austen, Anthony Trollope, and maybe Arthur Conan Doyle for 19th century morals and manners, plus H. G. Wells, and Jules Verne for retro-technological inspiration. Some of the latter can also be found in Alan Moore's *League of Extraordinary Gentlemen* as well as anime like the 2004 film *Steamboy* and the *Fullmetal Alchemist* tv series and movies. You might also find inspiration for characters and settings from Scott Westerfeld's steampunk trilogy of *Leviathan* novels and from Phil and Kaja Foglio's webcomic *Girl Genius*. A little further afield is Evelyn Waugh's *Brideshead Revisited*, which occurs mainly during the interwar period, but is still a good model for upper-class Britannic sensibilities. Of similar vintage but more comic and high-spirited is anything by P. G. Wodehouse (of Bertie Wooster and Jeeves fame). You can find many broadly drawn characters well worth stealing outright in his short stories about not-too-brainy bachelors trying to avoid the snares of matrimony and other inconveniences their relatives want to foist off on them. Agatha Christie is good for Edwardian mores and manners as well. In short, the game accommodates a wide range of fictional inspirations; bring in whatever makes the setting pop for you.

INNOCENTS ABROAD

The framework for the adventure involves the PCs enjoying a social season as guests and passengers—and possibly as servants or staff—aboard an airborne guesthouse called the Pension Bellevue. Beginning from Parisian moorings, it drifts to one *au courant* recreation after another, rendezvousing with other, similar establishments and the private aerial mansions of the very wealthy. The diversions available to the passengers aboard the Pension Bellevue include balls and receptions at which conversation and dancing will be much in evidence; outings to Italian opera houses and art museums, Gallic castles and wineries, and Roman ruins of all sorts, during which refined sensibilities and aesthetic tastes will show off to best advantage; and aerobatic sightseeing excursions over the countryside, requiring a deft hand on the piloting stick and a good sense of direction.

As they travel, the PCs become involved in a mix of romance, adventure, and high-stakes political intrigue. They may get into these tangles on their own, but some of their choices will be in response to the situations and complications that you, the GM, introduce. Here are some suggestions:

The Aerial Heiress: The PCs meet a beautiful foreign heiress, either a PC or NPC, whose patrimony in some wild region of the Caucasus is of strategic importance to the imperial ambitions of contending Great Powers. Were the girl properly submissive to the desires of her regal father, a regional potentate seeking to play the larger powers off against one another, she would be a mere pawn in the grand strategies of empire, to be married off to some princeling or other. However, with her Western education, she is headstrong, obstinate, and willful: she has decided that, if she is to marry, it will only be on her terms. She is willing to undertake any adventure—no matter how unwise, perilous, or foolhardy—if it offers but the slimmest chance of happiness.

Spy in the Sky: A Mata Hari-like spy from the Caliphate has infiltrated the Pension Bellevue, and she's well on her way to wheedling important Britannic secrets from a notable industrialist or scientist—perhaps someone whose interests one or more PCs are obliged to protect. Others may have reason to help her because they find the Britannic secrets reprehensible, fall in love with the winsome spy, or are susceptible to blackmail.

The Soft Crusade: An agent of the Pope has come from Novo Vaticano in Papal America to foment unrest and discord somewhere in the Old World, hoping to create an opportunity for the Supreme Pontiff's glorious return to European shores. To carry out his mission, he travels inconspicuously from city to city in a berth aboard the Pension Bellevue, using his cover as an itinerant scholar or crewmember to deflect attention or suspicion.

During any of these adventures, as the PCs go about their business, the tensions between the Great Powers that rule Europe will seethe and threaten to come to a head—putting pressure on the PCs, as their decisions and actions may influence the fate of Western civilization!

FATE: WORLDS OF ADVENTURE

A EUROPE THAT NEVER WAS

Before the game can commence in earnest, the players must be introduced to the setting. Let us imagine a late 19th century continent whose geopolitics are sufficiently familiar to be faithful to the period, but sufficiently original to allow for ahistorical action. Thus: a Plantagenet monarchy, in direct line from the Angevin Empire, covering most of Great Britain and continental France, with Germanic, Italian, and Iberian client states on its frontiers and colonies in the Americas, South Africa, and the Far East. Call this Britannia, presume that most PCs will belong to this nation, and give everyone there French-sounding names and English-sounding accents or vice versa. The backbone of Britannia's military is its fleet of mighty aerial dreadnoughts, and provisioning them necessitates far-flung refueling stops, including Gibraltar, Corsica, Algiers, Cairo, Crete, and Cyprus. Given this zealous and active program of foreign policy, the ambitions of Britannia's rivals threaten constant embarrassments.

Chief among these rivals is the Slavic power in the east that seeks to extend its influence further into the German principates, the Balkans, the Caucasus, and the Far East. Its armies consist chiefly of gigantic armored vehicles called juggernauts that rumble and clank across the battlefield. Call this the Muscovite Empire, with its ruler the Tsar, and consider it an implacable opponent of Britannia. Its emissaries and servitors bear Russian, Polish, and occasionally Germanic names, and they speak with Eastern European accents of various kinds. The fearsome Muscovite secret police serves the Tsar with ferocious zeal and ruthlessness, making Muscovy a byword for tyranny.

There is also a powerful but harried caliphate—not quite the "sick man of Europe," as with the 19th century Ottoman Empire, but still beset with numerous internal difficulties. Its leadership must manage a far-flung and ethnically diverse empire, and it is disinclined to take measures that might unduly upset the status quo. Nonetheless, it remains secure in its capital of Baghdad, itself a cosmopolitan center of culture and learning. It maintains its rule across Asia Minor and into the Balkans, across northern Africa and over to the Iberian Peninsula, into Ethiopia, and across Persia into the fierce Bactrian principalities on the western borders of India. Possessing such a wide swath of lands, the Caliphate can select and groom the most talented of its subjects for leadership. Its military force is smaller and less technologically sophisticated than those of its rivals, but its artillery is known as the finest in the world, drawing upon a long tradition of mathematical and technical excellence. The city-busting siege mortars of the Caliph's Household Guard are particularly feared.

GMs, you could just describe all this to the players, but in the spirit of the Bronze Rule—the idea that *anything* can be a character under the right circumstances—why not introduce players to the setting by having them play it out?

The Balance of Power

Before playing at the level of individual characters, play a round or two acting out the grand strategic maneuvering of the Great Powers. Break up the players into three teams—one each for Britannia, the Muscovite Empire, and the Caliphate of Baghdad—and allow each Power to take an action on its turn. If there are more than three players, put the excess on the Britannia team to encourage later patriotism. They could also play minor countries. You'll find character sheets for the three Great Powers on page 11. Each team gets one action per exchange and can spend a fate point to get a second action. Besides giving a sense of the setting, the Great Powers game will produce aspects that can be invoked once the game focuses down to the character level.

The map below shows the three Great Powers as well as neutral nations and client states. The unaligned nations include Portugal, Switzerland, Denmark, the Kingdom of Naples, and the Holy Roman Empire. British clients and possessions include the Kingdom of Leon and Castile, the Kingdom of Italy, the Kingdom of Norway, the Kingdom of Jerusalem and its surrounding fiefs—also known as Outremer—and many German principalities. Muscovite clients include Sweden, Poland, eastern Germany including Prussia, a swath of minor potentates in the Caucasus, and the broad Cossack-swept steppes east of the Caspian Sea. The Caliphate doesn't have true client states, but the provincial governors on its frontiers amount to semi-independent rulers in their own right under the nominal overlordship of the Caliph; particularly potent are the Emir of Tunis, on the North African coast south of Sicily, and the Sultan of Istanbul, where the Black Sea meets the Mediterranean.

Great Powers and Minor Countries

Each Great Power has three aspects: its high concept, a color (flavor) aspect, and an internal trouble aspect. A Great Power also has four skills: Diplomacy, Espionage, Industry, and Warfare, described in greater detail on the next page. Each Great Power begins with 1 free stunt and 3 refresh, and they can trade refresh for stunts as in *Fate Core*. They have two stress tracks, political and military, each starting with 2 stress boxes. Diplomacy gives more political stress boxes, and Warfare gives more military stress boxes: +1 box for Great (+4), +2 boxes for Superb (+5).

Political stress reflects the internal stability and national will of the country. When a Great Power or minor country is taken out politically, it can do one of two things: escalate to military conflict with one or more of its neighbors, or undergo a coup, revolution, or civil war. The former requires the Great Power use Warfare to attack an enemy at least once; the latter requires the Great Power to rewrite its high concept, approved by the GM. In either case its political stress is completely renewed, whether by going through a constitutional crisis or coming face-to-face with an external foe.

Military stress reflects the strength and good order of the Great Power's armed forces. When a Great Power is taken out militarily, it surrenders unconditionally. If this happens, the victor can rewrite the Great Power's aspects, redistribute its skills, and remove any or all of its existing stunts, which restores its refresh. This is a game changer! Think Treaty of Versailles: reparations, indemnities, and generations-long resentments seething until they produce even more brutal warfare and crueler internal policies. An aerial excursion under these conditions may be fraught with let-them-eat-cake obliviousness or earnest misery tourism.

Each minor country, whether headed by a PC or NPC, gets three aspects as described for the Great Powers, one Good (+3) skill, one Fair (+2) skill, one Average (+1) skill, and one Mediocre (+0) skill. Minor countries get no free stunts and 3 refresh. If you have major time constraints—running the game in a four-hour convention slot, for example—you should probably avoid writing up all this for minor countries. Remember that the Great Power game, as fun and engaging as most players will find it, is not the focus of the adventure.

Great Power Skills

Diplomacy

The conduct of foreign policy by negotiating, treaty-making, and otherwise influencing the policies and intentions of another power.

Overcome: Use Diplomacy to overcome the recalcitrance or reluctance of foreign powers, gain the compliance of neutral nations and client states, and smooth over potential diplomatic incidents. For example, if a neutral nation is reluctant to allow foreign troops on its territory, careful diplomacy might ease their concerns.

Create an Advantage: Use Diplomacy to create advantageous diplomatic agreements and understandings, producing aspects like *International Good Will* or *Trade Agreement*.

Attack: Diplomacy can be used to inflict political stress upon an enemy, representing the use of propaganda, bluster, high-level denunciations, ultimatums, and similar pronouncements, as well as trade sanctions and other non-military action.

Defend: Use Diplomacy to defend against diplomatic attacks.

Espionage

Intelligence gathering by deploying spies, recruiting and using secret agents for covert missions, and employing other tools of international subterfuge.

Overcome: Espionage can be used to ferret out enemy secrets and plans, as well as to deal with problems related to intelligence, spying, and more generally knowledge of the enemy's intentions and capabilities. Overcoming using Espionage can temporarily neutralize a foe's aspect or even, if you succeed with style, give you a free invocation on it. For example, if Muscovite spies smuggled out the patrol routes of Britannic aerial dreadnoughts, then **Britannia Rules the Skies** could be regarded as an empty boast, at least until Britannic counter-intelligence secured the leak by succeeding on its own overcome action. Until then, Britannia couldn't invoke the aspect against Muscovy, and if the Espionage action succeeded with style, the Tsar of Muscovy could invoke it once for free.

Create an Advantage: Espionage can be used to plant disinformation and otherwise mislead the enemy. It can create advantages like **Political Unrest** in the enemy camp, a **Fifth Column** of covert operatives in an enemy country, and so forth.

Attack: Espionage can be used to inflict political stress upon an enemy, representing sabotage, terrorism, and fifth-column attacks.

Defend: Use Espionage for counter-intelligence; that is, attempts to defend against foreign espionage efforts. It can also be used to defend against diplomatic attacks, representing intelligence about the enemy's true intentions and capabilities as well as covert operations against their diplomatic personnel.

Industry

The economic and industrial resources under the Great Power's command, including its scientific and technological wherewithal.

 Overcome: Production in the Great Power's factories lets it deal with problems and difficulties related to military materiel, industrial capacity, and economic strength. Technological innovations and scientific breakthroughs may help overcome complex problems produced by political, economic, and empirical constraints. For example, if a Great Power were suffering *Communications Difficulties* because of imperial overstretch, it might devote its industry to laying sturdy telegraph cables across its frontiers, enabling faster and more reliable communication with outlying provinces. Industry can also restore ranks in Warfare as it degrades (see below). The passive opposition to restoring Warfare ranks equals the current Warfare rank; success restores one lost rank, and success with style restores two.

 Create an Advantage: Economic development and technical innovation can enable a Great Power to gain advantages over its enemies. The benefits of material prosperity and abundance may be distributed widely across a society or appropriated by its elites. Some of these advantages can be invoked for stunt-like effects; for example, *Strategic Bombing* might allow Industry to be used to attack.

Attack: Industry is not typically used to attack.

Defend: Industry is not typically used to defend.

Warfare

The maneuvering of armies, navies, and aerial fleets against an enemy. Each time Warfare is used to attack or defend, it **degrades** by one rank. Lost ranks of Warfare can be restored by overcoming using Industry (see above), by spending fate points (restores one Warfare rank per fate point), or by invoking a relevant aspect (restores two ranks).

Overcome: Military action can overcome obstacles related to the presence of opposing military forces or disadvantageous situation aspects.

Create an Advantage: Military maneuvering creates battlefield advantages—for example, surrounding or besieging an opposing force, fixing or screening enemy forces, or forcing enemies to maneuver out of position.

Attack: Direct military action inflicts military stress on an enemy. An enemy who is taken out by military means sues for peace.

Defend: Warfare is used to defend against military attacks.

The Great Powers

Britannia

High Concept: *Steam-Powered, Anglo-French Victorian Empire*
Color Aspect: *Britannia Rules the Skies*
Internal Trouble: *Public-Spirited Egalitarian Reform Movements*

Skills

Diplomacy: Good (+3)   **Industry:** Superb (+5)
Espionage: Fair (+2)   **Warfare:** Great (+4)

Stunts

Britannia Expects That Every Man Shall Do His Duty: Once per session, if you have used Warfare to attack or defend, you can invoke ***Britannia Rules the Skies*** for free.

Stress

Political ☐☐   **Military** ☐☐☐

Refresh: 3

Muscovite Empire

High Concept: *Cruel and Authoritarian Tsarist Autocracy*
Color Aspect: *Do Not Provoke the Juggernaut!*
Internal Trouble: *Anarcho-Syndicalist Conspirators*

Skills

Diplomacy: Fair (+2)   **Industry:** Good (+3)
Espionage: Great (+4)   **Warfare:** Superb (+5)

Stunts

Tsar's Secret Police: If an enemy attempts to use Espionage to create an advantage against you by infiltrating foreign agents into the Muscovite Empire, you gain +2 to defend against it.

General Winter: If an opponent attacks you with Warfare, and they caused you to take at least one military stress from defending against their Warfare attack in your most recent exchange with them, you may spend a fate point to require that opponent to degrade his Warfare score by two ranks instead of one. Remember, only a fool gets involved in a land war in Asia.

Stress

Political ☐☐   **Military** ☐☐☐☐

Refresh: 2

Caliphate of Baghdad

High Concept: *Subtle and Urbane yet Despotic Imperium*
Color Aspect: *Baghdad, the Ancient and Sublime City*
Internal Trouble: *Nationalist Factions in Far-Off Corners*

Skills

Diplomacy: Superb (+5) **Industry:** Fair (+2)
Espionage: Great (+4) **Warfare:** Good (+3)

Stunts

Treasure Trove of History: When defending against a Warfare attack, you may spend a fate point and describe the ancient historical site in your lands. If you do, your opponent must take care to avoid damaging this site irrevocably in his attack. If your opponent exercises due care, he must reduce his Warfare by 2 for the current attack. Otherwise, he must mark his lowest unmarked political stress box.

Janissaries: Because you command a secretive martial order of infiltrators, you can attack with Espionage to inflict military stress. When doing so, your Espionage degrades as if it were Warfare, and is restored the same way.

Crossroads of the World: Because of your location astride the major trade routes of the world, you can use Diplomacy in place of Industry to overcome obstacles related to accessing rare or scarce resources.

Stress

Political ☐☐☐☐ Military ☐☐
Refresh: 1

Opening Salvos

Before you zoom in on the characters, begin the Great Power game with a situation tied into the plot that you expect to run at the character level. Here are some examples. Though they are not capitalized like aspects, anything here written in *aspect style* is indeed an aspect you can use.

The Aerial Heiress: A small Caucasian principality called the Emirate of Azeria—situated about where Azerbaijan would be in our world—has discovered *large coal deposits* that could make it an important way station for Britannic airships en route to India, and its *ambitious potentate* has made overtures to British representatives regarding the possibility of an alliance. To seal the deal, he has a *marriageable daughter* that he is willing to wed to a suitably aristocratic husband. However, the Tsar regards the area as part of the *Muscovite sphere of influence*, and *the caliph is wary* of both Britannic encroachment and Muscovite adventurism on his borders, seeing them as threats to the status quo that could lead to political instability within the Caliphate itself.

Spy in the Sky: A *consortium of Britannic industrialists* has convinced the Admiralty to embark upon an ambitious program to upgrade the aerial fleet with *a new class of super-dreadnoughts* currently on the drawing boards that incorporate *top-secret scientific breakthroughs* in their design. An *outraged and vocal minority* of the Britannic public regards the development as an unnecessary and supremely expensive provocation, and the ambassadors of the Tsar and the Caliph have both voiced *strenuous diplomatic objections* to the project.

The Soft Crusade: A *wave of religious fervor* coming from the members of the traditionally Catholic working class in the neutral Kingdom of Naples has spread to Caliphate possessions in Greece and the Mediterranean, provoking *protests, demonstrations, and violence*. Provincial governors within the Caliphate have undertaken *brutal repressive measures*, and *public opinion in Britannia is aghast* at some of the reports coming from abroad. Within the Kingdom of Naples, there is now an *increasingly emboldened religious movement* raising *strong hopes for the Pope's return from Papal America* to Italian shores.

GMs, if you are sufficiently confident in your ability to improvise, throw all three scenarios into the mix and see what develops. Allow the situation to develop a little bit—perhaps the Powers will vie for advantage, or maybe someone will launch an overwhelming military strike. Freeze the action when things seem poised to develop further, but well before they are fully resolved. For example:

The Aerial Heiress: Britannia develops the Emir of Azeria's coal deposits against the Tsar's strong protests (Industry), while Muscovy masses troops on the border (Warfare, unopposed), and the Caliphate works against Britannia's counterintelligence efforts to entice the daughter into a love affair with a handsome Caliphate artillery officer (Espionage).

Spy in the Sky: Britannia moves forward with its plans to build the super-dreadnoughts (Industry), while the Caliph calls for tri-lateral disarmament talks (Diplomacy), and the Muscovite Empire sends secret agents to infiltrate the naval construction sites and sabotage the new vessels (Espionage).

The Soft Crusade: The Caliphate deploys its Janissaries to disperse protestors in several locations (Espionage, used as Warfare), while Britannia sends humanitarian aid to the affected regions to calm things down (Diplomacy). The Tsar takes advantage of his rivals' pre-occupation by sending troops into a disputed border region (Warfare, unopposed).

After a round or two of the Great Power game, tell the players in your most judicious tone that, now that they know generally what's going on in the world, it's time to zoom in to the character game. Any aspects or other consequences established by the Great Powers remain in play as appropriate. Again, be conscious of time—one round is usually enough to get players engaged with the setting. You can promise them you'll play more of the Great Power game at some point, which we recommend if you want more inspiration or complications for character-level play.

The Pension Bellevue

As players create characters, lay out the Pension Bellevue blueprint found below as well as the aerial route map and the list of potential PCs and NPCs in the *"Dramatis Personae"* starting on page 17. Explain that the game will begin with the PCs embarked upon the Pension Bellevue, an ***Elegant, Old-Fashioned Sky-Salon*** scheduled for an extended tour of the continent. It will float in the skies above Britannia and its neighbors, pushed by wind-sail and steam propeller, visiting romantic and picturesque destinations across Europe and beyond to rendezvous with similar excursions for social occasions and revelry. The PCs have, for one reason or another, chosen to be aboard the Pension Bellevue as it makes its way across the skies. For a more rules-heavy description of the Pension Bellevue, consult the *Extra: Vehicles* chapter starting on page 34.

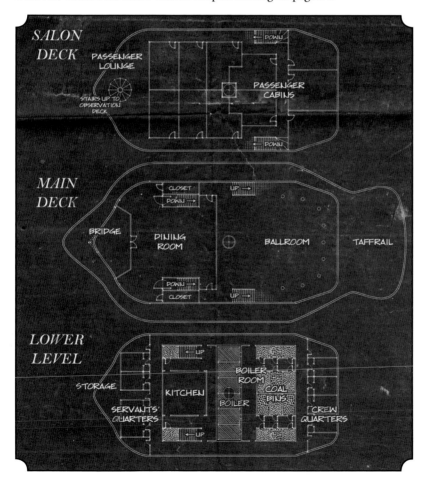

Creating Characters

Provide the *"Dramatis Personae"* (page 17) to the players. They may be inspired to create new characters that contrast or fit in with the listed characters in interesting ways, or they may find listed characters congenial to their interests. Either is appropriate. Alternately, the Great Power game may provide ideas for characters. In any case, creating a character follows the same steps: create character aspects, select skills, and choose some stunts.

Aspects

Each PC gets 5 aspects that define his or her place in the game.

High Concept: This is a brief phrase that describes your character in broad terms. If you want, you can base these on the two-word descriptions from the Dramatis Personae. Example: You might choose to play Yves Chevalier, the **Bombastic Industrialist**.

Place in Society: This reflects your character's status in Britannic society. It may reference the particular social set or circle to which your character belongs or the attitude toward or perspective on "polite society" he or she holds. This can be used to establish subtle or not-so-subtle contrasts or extensions of your high concept. Example: You might decide that Chevalier is in fact a **West Indian Provincial Parvenu**, letting you indulge a desire to play a person of color in a 19th century drawing room fantasy.

Place Aboard: This reflects your character's relationship to the Pension Bellevue, his or her reason for being aboard, whether as paying passenger, part of the ship's crew, or servant to one of the travelers. Example: ***"I'm paying for all of this, my good man!"*** would suggest that Chevalier is bankrolling the excursion for himself and possibly several other guests.

Desire: This reflects what your character wants from others, whether PCs or NPCs. The desire may be sincerely matrimonial or more mercenary, or it may reflect your character's ambitions for social approval, professional success, or financial security. Example: ***"Professor Arroget's formula will make us both rich!"*** points Chevalier at the good professor with the intention of using Arroget's knowledge for business purposes.

Refusal: Another PC or NPC wants something from your character, and this aspect reflects why your character won't or can't give it to them. Example: Mme. Duchamp has the aspect ***"My daughter would do well to wed Mr. Chevalier."*** Mr. Chevalier could have the refusal aspect ***"I want a woman who gives as good as she gets."*** since Camille Duchamp, the daughter, is described as a sad-eyed poetess, which implies that she is a little too meek and retiring for Chevalier.

This aspect could be useful for pushing Chevalier at a more outspoken character, such as Mademoiselle Chandru. Meanwhile, Professor Arroget might respond to Chevalier's importunings with a refusal aspect such as ***"The purity of science is sacrosanct!"***, reflecting that he's unwilling to share the formula that Chevalier needs. Multiple characters might want something from your character, but he or she still only gets a single refusal aspect—best write it broadly!

In play, when a desire is definitively obtained or a refusal is complete and irreversible, rewrite the corresponding aspect immediately. For example, if Monsieur Chevalier became engaged to Mademoiselle Chandru, Madame Duchamp would be within her rights to change her desire aspect to something like ***"Mr. Chevalier will pay for this insult!"***. Mr. Chevalier, now betrothed to a woman who gives as good as she gets, might change his refusal aspect to something like ***"Be careful what you wish for."***

Skills, Refresh and Stunts
Each PC gets one Great (+4) skill, two Good (+3) skills, three Fair (+2) skills, and four Average (+1) skills. We use a different skill list from the *Fate Core System*; find it on page 21. The PCs each get 3 free stunts and 3 refresh, and they can trade refresh for stunts on a one-to-one basis. A PC's Will determines his or her mental stress track, as in *Fate Core*. Some particularly rich characters may have a financial stress track as an extra. This is described under the Business skill (page 22). Unlike in *Fate Core*, characters do not have a physical stress track. Instead, they roll dice to withstand injury as described under the Physique skill (page 22).

Dramatis Personae
On the next two pages are 16 potential characters that players can adopt wholesale, draw inspiration from, or use as foils, friends, rivals, and enemies in creating their own characters. They each have two aspects, a high concept and what amounts to a refusal aspect, and two skills. If you run any as NPCs, you can flesh them out with additional aspects and supplement their skills either by adding one Fair (+2) skill and one Average (+1) skill or by giving them full skill pyramids. Players, you can use these as PCs, adapting and modifying their aspects and skills as you wish.

Mlle. Natalie Gaudan

Flirtatious Nymphet *Vivacious but Vain*
Skills: Great (+4) Deceive, Good (+3) Perform

Mlle. Aimee Bourg

Discreet Maid *Clever Beyond Her Years*
Skills: Great (+4) Empathy, Good (+3) Notice

Mlle. Elodie Prideaux

Discerning Governess
Taste-Conscious and Fashionable
Skills: Great (+4) Converse, Good (+3) Society

Mlle. Camille Duchamp

Sad-Eyed Poetess *A Fading Rose*
Skills: Great (+4) Perform, Good (+3) Converse

Mlle. Talia Chandru

Wealthy Foreign Heiress *She's So Modern*
Skills: Great (+4) Will, Good (+3) Business

Mme. Adela Arroget

Giddy Matron *"Oh, my husband knows a
trick worth two of that!"*
Skills: Great (+4) Converse, Good (+3) Perform

Mme. Bridget Duchamp

Fretful Widow *"What's to become of
my daughter?"*
Skills: Great (+4) Empathy, Good (+3) Society

Dame Ada Desmarais

Blue-Blooded Matriarch *Knows What's Good
for Everybody*
Skills: Great (+4) Society, Good (+3) Provoke

Mr. Rene Balmer
Sophomoric Undergraduate   *Fond of Japes*
Skills: Great (+4) Deceive, Good (+3) Provoke

Mr. Jean-Paul Aloysien
Handsome Aero-Chaffeur   *Earnest but Diffident*
Skills: Great (+4) Pilot, Good (+3) Physique

Capt. Thibault Nerond
Stylish Sky-Hussar   *Prickly Sense of Honor*
Skills: Great (+4) Shoot, Good (+3) Athletics

Col. Henri Bose-Batonne
Supercilious Martinet   *Cashiered for Dueling*
Skills: Great (+4) Command, Good (+3) Fight

Mr. Yves Chevalier
Bombastic Industrialist   *Hearty Appetite*
Skills: Great (+4) Business, Good (+3) Provoke

Dr. Pascal Gravois
Kindly Physician   *Knows More Than He Lets On*
Skills: Great (+4) Scholarship, Good (+3) Notice

Prof. Raymond Arroget
Brilliant Academician   *Encyclopedic Mind*
Skills: Great (+4) Scholarship, Good (+3) Society

Ambassador Heinrich Dunkelfeld
Diplomat from Muscovite Puppet State   *Fond of the Ladies*
Skills: Great (+4) Deceit, Good (+3) Converse

POINT THE PCS AT EACH OTHER

GMs, you will have less work to do if the PCs are each other's objects of desire and refusal. This is not a hard-and-fast rule, since you will also want NPCs motivated to make trouble for the PCs by virtue of their refusal aspects, but you'll be kept busy enough by managing the overarching plot of rising Great Power tensions and by providing the details of the Pension Bellevue's journey.

There are a number of options to entwine the PCs. If your players are not the sort to automatically aim their ambitions at each other, consider requiring the players to direct their desire aspect toward the player to their right and their refusal aspect toward the player to their left. Include yourself in that circle if you so choose. Alternately, see what the players produce on their own, and suggest modifications and alterations so that, when you map out the links created by desires and refusals, you can trace a route from any PC to any other.

If needed, introduce an NPC or two to "complete the circuit" or complicate the relationship map. If you are running **The Aerial Heiress**, for example, include both Mlle. Chandru, the Azerian heiress whose inheritance represents a strategic advantage to the Great Powers, and Ambassador Dunkelfeld, the Prussian diplomat secretly in service to Muscovite masters. If you use a different plot hook, add other NPCs. For **Spy in the Sky**, Mademoiselle Gaudan would make a fine spy trying to winkle the blueprints that Monsieur Chevalier is carrying, or the war plans that Colonel Bose-Batonne is drafting for the Admiralty. For **The Soft Crusade**, Monsieur Aloysien or Professor Arroget would each serve as a capable *agent provocateur* for the Pope—or perhaps they are working together.

Non-Player Characters

Any characters not chosen by the players become NPCs. If a player references an NPC in a desire or refusal aspect, consider fleshing him or her out a little more fully with additional aspects and skills. Otherwise, the descriptions in the *"Dramatis Personae"* (page 17) should provide enough information for characterizing and playing NPCs. Allow them to come and go at need, complicating the PCs' lives with their enthusiasms, desires, and importunings. Deft improvisation is your watchword!

SKILLS

This skill list replaces the list in *Fate Core*.

Athletics: Per *Fate Core*. Includes the ability to dance, ride, and otherwise engage in vigorous outdoor sporting activities, including archery.

Business (new): Practical knowledge of speculation, investment, and related financial matters. Business combines those parts of Resources and Contacts related to knowledge of and ability to function within the dog-eat-dog world of business, as opposed to the world of formal social relations.

Command (new): The ability to lead and inspire; charisma more generally. Subsumes that part of Rapport.

Converse (new): The ability to make oneself agreeable in company of a suitable social standing. Subsumes that part of Rapport.

Deceive: Per *Fate Core*—but beware, lest one be taken for a cad and a bounder!

Drive: Per *Fate Core*. If you wish to operate Muscovite juggernauts and Britannic steam engines, you'll need this.

Empathy: Per *Fate Core*.

Fight: Per *Fate Core*. It includes fencing training and (illegal) dueling experience, as well as fisticuffs and brawling.

Gamble (new): Knowledge of betting tables, horse races, and all card games more vicious than a rubber of whist.

Investigate: Per *Fate Core*.

Mechanics (modified): Replaces Crafts. It is used to maintain and repair aeroplanes and airships, as well as other steam-powered devices.

Notice: Per *Fate Core*. It also includes aesthetic appreciation—the ability to attend to and evaluate an artistic performance, in other words.

Perform (new): The ability to sing, recite poetry or oratorical compositions, play a musical instrument, or draw—all particularly expected of young ladies. Perform represents a well-rounded artistic education; to reflect a talent in a particular kind of performance, take a Perform stunt. This skill might also be used to represent any handicraft not comfortably situated in Mechanics, such as sewing, cooking, and forging official documents.

Physique (modified): Per *Fate Core*. Characters do not have a physical stress track. Instead, they use Physique to overcome the damage inflicted by a physical attack; failure indicates injury, unconsciousness, or death. For example, if a Fight attack achieves a Fair (+2) result, the target of that attack must use Physique to overcome a Fair obstacle. If the target fails, she is taken out. These rules make physical combat very brief, a punctuation mark rather than an extended sentence in the sequence of play.

Pilot (new): The ability to handle an aerial machine with equanimity. It operates much the same as Drive.

Provoke: Per *Fate Core*. Appropriate for curmudgeonly aunts and scurrilous editors.

Scholarship (modified): Replaces Lore. Indicates formal education. Scholarship stunts can be used to reflect specialized legal or medical training.

Shoot: Per *Fate Core*, though dueling is outlawed. Refers specifically to gunplay; archery is part of Athletics. It also includes the ability to operate heavy gunnery on vehicles.

Society (modified): Replaces Contacts. Includes knowledge of etiquette and formal social rules appropriate to your position and place in society, subsuming that part of Rapport.

Stealth: Per *Fate Core*, but also includes actions originally covered by Burglary.

Will: Per *Fate Core*.

Business

This is practical knowledge of the world of business. It includes the ability to make money by means of investments, lending at interest, issuing stock or other certificates of ownership, and similar financial maneuvering, as well as by running a shop or other commercial enterprise. While it includes the conduct of business dealings, negotiations, and sales pitches, it only applies to professional or commercial transactions, not interpersonal or social encounters, which are the province of Converse, Society, and similar skills.

Overcome: Business can be used to overcome obstacles related to running a business, such as finding suppliers or sources of raw materials, dealing with labor problems or recalcitrant workers, handling business-related legal issues, and so forth. You can use Business to reduce your wealth stress (see next page) against passive opposition equal to the value of the stress box to be recovered.

Create an Advantage: Business advantages usually reflect profitable commercial ventures coming to fruition, so aspects such as ***Return on Investment*** or ***Got in on the Ground Floor*** are reasonable.

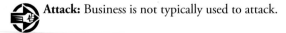 **Attack:** Business is not typically used to attack.

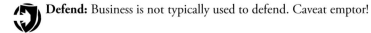 **Defend:** Business is not typically used to defend. Caveat emptor!

Extra: Wealth

Permissions: An aspect related to wealth or economic status
Costs: Skill ranks, if you want permanent financial stress boxes

Most characters don't have much disposable income, regardless of rank or status. They are more or less secure in their living—either from inherited or acquired wealth or by virtue of their employment, unless they have an aspect or consequence indicating otherwise—but they are typically without large reserves of liquidity. However, in this quasi-Victorian age, there do exist characters of great wealth, either old-money nobility or *nouveau riche* arrivistes.

To represent great wealth, a PC can gain ranks in Wealth. However, Wealth is not used as a normal skill. Instead, each rank in Wealth adds one financial stress box with a value equal to the rank just taken; for example, Good (+3) Wealth gives three financial stress boxes with values of 1, 2, and 3. These boxes can be marked to do one of two things: absorb shifts of damage equal to the value of the box, or add a bonus to an action using another skill, with a rank equal to or less than Wealth, equal to the value of the box, to a maximum of +3. In both cases, the use of wealth must be appropriate for the circumstances, where bringing economic resources to bear on a problem, situation, or action would help produce a satisfying outcome.

Wealth is fungible in a way that other parts of a character are not. A character can give a financial stress box to another character, who then "owns" it. Once it is used, the character who first owned the financial stress box can restore it by using an overcome action, usually Business, possibly Society or Gamble, or perhaps even something further afield like Perform or Scholarship under the right conditions. This action has passive opposition equal to the value of the financial stress box to be restored.

Even a character *without* Wealth can try to raise money by rolling an action to gain some temporary wealth: an aspect reflecting the nature of the financial resource (such as **Selling the Family Jewels**) and a financial stress box. Succeeding gives a 2-point financial stress box, while succeeding with style gives a 3-point box. The passive opposition to this roll should be at least Good (+3), possibly higher, since making money is hard. See the discussion about wagers under the Gamble skill on page 27.

These rules make characters without Wealth more vulnerable to economic pressure or financial adversity than characters with Wealth. In such cases, the pressure or adversity will be experienced as either disadvantageous aspects or as attacks inflicting mental stress.

Business Stunts

Let's Make a Deal: You can use Business in place of Converse or Society to interact with others as long as you frame the encounter as some quid pro quo exchange.

Collateral: Gain an additional mild consequence slot, used to absorb mental or financial stress from economic adversity.

Command

This is your ability to inspire loyalty and effectively direct others' performance, particularly subordinates and more generally those inclined to defer to your authority.

 Overcome: Use Command to motivate reluctant or flagging subordinates, rally wavering troops, or smarten up the household staff.

 Create an Advantage: Command can create advantages reflecting the quality of inspired or highly motivated subordinates, companions, underlings, or staff.

 Attack: Command is not typically used to attack, although in certain mass combat situations you can use it to lead troops against a defending force.

 Defend: Command is not typically used to defend, although in certain mass combat situations you can use it to lead troops against an attacking force.

Extra: Troops and Crew

Permissions: An aspect indicating that you are an officer in Britannic service or otherwise hold authority over some body of troops or the crew of a vessel.

Costs: Refresh, if you want the troops or crew to have skills

Troops or crew are defined by a high concept, usually the name of their unit or another designation, such as *1st Battalion, King's Royal Riflemen* or *HMS Valiant Crew*. They begin with no skills, but you can spend refresh to give them a skill stack with a peak skill equal to the refresh that you spent—for example, spending 3 refresh gives them one Good (+3) skill, one Fair (+2) skill, and one Average (+1) skill. They will take action as you direct. They start with 2 unit stress boxes, reflecting unit cohesion, and increases with Will, representing unit morale. Good (+3) or Great (+4) Will gives 3 stress boxes, Superb (+5) or Fantastic (+6) Will gives 4 stress boxes, and so forth. Only enemies of comparable numbers can inflict stress upon troops or crew, so a lone character usually cannot. However, a single individual may be able to temporarily discomfit a body of troops or evade them.

Sample Troops

Muscovite Shock Troops (**3 refresh**): Good (+3) Morale, Fair (+2) Shoot, Average (+1) Fight. Unit Stress: ☐☐☐
Muscovite Cossack Cavalry Squadron (**3 refresh**): Good (+3) Ride, Fair (+2) Fight, Average (+1) Shoot. Unit Stress: ☐☐
Caliphate Artillery Battery (**3 refresh**): Good (+3) Mechanics, Fair (+2) Shoot, Average (+1) Drive. Unit Stress: ☐☐
Caliphate Janissary Battalion (**4 refresh**): Great (+4) Stealth, Good (+3) Fight, Fair (+2) Morale, Average (+1) Shoot. Unit Stress: ☐☐
Britannic Regular Infantry Company (**3 refresh**): Good (+3) Shoot, Fair (+2) Morale, Average (+1) Athletics. Unit Stress: ☐☐

Command Stunts

Unflappable: Your air of authority makes you difficult to faze. You can use Command in place of Will to defend or overcome in stressful situations where you can fall back on your formal position or the performance of your duties. For example, if you have taken charge of an airship while it is under attack, and the attackers try to intimidate you into striking your colors—attacking you to inflict mental stress—instead of defending with Will to keep your morale steady, you can defend with Command.

Here Comes the Cavalry!: You can spend a fate point to have your troops rendezvous with you per retroactively transmitted orders, showing up in circumstances when they would otherwise be too far away to assist you.

Converse

This is your ability to "be agreeable in company"—to come across as personable, affable, and even charming when interacting with social acquaintances. It's also how effective you are at self-expression and social interaction more generally, though it is more limited than Rapport in *Fate Core*: strictly speaking, interaction across lines of class and status is governed by Society, while the ability to lead and inspire is governed by Command.

 Overcome: You can use agreeable conversation to smooth over difficulties related to the standoffishness of your interlocutors or the awkwardness of your social position. You can also use Converse to woo someone.

 Create an Advantage: You can use Converse to create advantages related to leaving favorable impressions upon acquaintances or extracting information from conversation. You can also impart information to an acquaintance and expect it to become common knowledge after a short time—a few days at worst to a few hours under ideal conditions. Depending on the sort of information being bruited—gossip, rumors, or slanderous accusations, for example—this may create an aspect or just establish a disadvantageous fictional situation for the character.

Attack: Converse is generally not used to attack; use Provoke instead.

Defend: Converse is generally not used to defend; use Deceive instead.

Converse Stunts

Vicious Gossip: You can use Converse to attack someone in your social circle by spreading malicious gossip about them, as long as the rumor you are spreading is true insofar as you can determine. If you succeed, you inflict mental stress. If you want to lie about them, use Deceive instead.

Gamble

This represents your skill and experience with games of chance, including cards and dice, as well as your knowledge of horse racing and blood sports of all sorts. Aboard ship, innocent card games are often transformed into low-stakes gambling, and passengers have been known to bet on the weather and the number of passing aircraft (or birds!) they will encounter over a certain period. Most of the time, such things are merely color, part and parcel of conversation aboard ship. However, when stakes are higher, Gamble can be used to overcome obstacles and create advantages.

Overcome: Use Gamble to overcome problems related to knowing the odds and making the appropriate bet. You can also use it to detect attempts at cheating such as marked cards, loaded dice, and similar stratagems.

Create an Advantage: Use Gamble to create advantages related to winning at a game of chance, such as *Vingt-et-Un Winnings* or *Deed to Old Rowleigh's Mill*, or to create a wager for high-stakes play (page 28).

Attack: Gamble is not typically used to attack, but a high-stakes game may put one's nerves under stress, as his or her fortune may indeed be on the line. In such circumstances, Gamble can used to attack in order to inflict mental stress.

Defend: Gamble is not typically used to defend.

High-Stakes Gambling

In high-stakes play, each side stakes a wager consisting of an aspect and a **stakes value**. This wager can be represented by staking Wealth, with a stakes value equal to the value of the financial stress box staked. Alternatively, a character can create an advantage to garner stakes for the wager; succeeding yields an aspect with a stakes value of 2, succeeding with style yields one with a stakes value of 3. For example, a character could use Business to sell off some land or use Society to touch up some friends for cash, creating the wager *Pile of Cash*. Characters involved in the high-stakes play roll Gamble; the highest roll wins, gaining a temporary extra financial stress box of the highest stakes value among the wagers while retaining their own; the others lose their wagers. See the discussion of Wealth on page 23.

Under some circumstances, high-stakes gambling becomes an outright conflict, with the wagers remaining on the table until all but one gambler is taken out or concedes. During such a conflict, the gamblers can use Notice, Deceive, Empathy, and Converse as well as Gamble and Will in order to attack and defend.

Gamble Stunts

Poker Face: You can use Gamble in place of Deceive to bluff, stonewall, or otherwise rely on hiding your true intentions or disposition while interacting with others.

Winnings: You can spend a fate point to produce wealth, representing previous winnings. Each fate point you spend in this way creates a 2-point financial stress box and an aspect like *Cold Hard Cash* or *Ready Money*. See the discussion of Wealth on page 23.

Mechanics

This represents your general mechanical aptitude and training. It also includes your ability to manipulate the rigging and fittings of a craft to adjust its speed, trim, and altitude.

Overcome: Use Mechanics to overcome difficulties related to the mechanical operability of equipment and vehicles by making sure they work and stay in good repair. It is also useful for overcoming difficulties created by in-flight conditions aboard an airship.

Create an Advantage: Given appropriate tools and enough time, Mechanics can be used to create helpful machines that assist in completing physical tasks. It can also be used to reflect the speedy, precise completion of aerial ship-handling tasks.

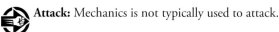 **Attack:** Mechanics is not typically used to attack.

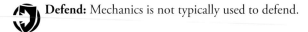 **Defend:** Mechanics is not typically used to defend.

Mechanics Stunts

Crack Airman: +2 to Mechanics when dealing with the routine mechanical tasks related to keeping an airship flying.

Inventor: Once per session, you can spend a fate point to introduce a useful mechanical contraption that is bulky, noisy, and connected to a limited or otherwise restrictive power supply. Define the invention as an aspect that includes its limitations: for example, ***Clanking Steam-Powered Calculating Machine***. If the GM allows, you can add additional elements to your invention, making it a true extra.

Powered by Steam!

Characters with knowledge of Mechanics will be at least somewhat familiar with the workings and nomenclature of steam power. A strong and sturdy boiler contains liquid, usually water, supplied from a tank via a pump called an injector. The water is heated by a motor unit or firebox, which burns coal, wood, or oil delivered by hand or mechanical stoker from a storage bunker. This process creates steam which typically drives a set of pistons, which in turn moves a crankshaft and flywheel, which—when connected via mechanical linkages such as gears, cogs, and reciprocating rods—operates various sorts of machinery. The steam may be vented in billowing plumes, or recovered via condensers that siphon liquid back to the water tank.

Such complicated machinery will inevitably develop mechanical problems. Represent these as aspects the GM can compel when the characters operate steam-powered equipment. GMs, you can create these aspects to add mechanical complications to the ongoing action—for example, as might happen if the Pension Bellevue were pursued by sky pirates or if a PC aeroplane pilot pushed her craft to the limit and succeeded at a cost. If you want to randomly generate a mechanical problem aspect, roll two fate dice and pick from the following table:

Roll	Mechanical Problem
⊟⊟	*Boiler Pressure Low*
■⊟	*Leaky Valve Fittings*
⊟⊞	*Firebox Not Drawing*
■■	*Loose Gears*
■⊞	*Injector Pump Malfunction*
⊞⊞	*Pressure Build-Up!*

The consequences of mechanical failure may include work stoppage, damage to the equipment, and injury to the operator; the unexpected venting of superheated steam can scald the unwary in horrific ways. Sometimes a mechanic must expose him or herself to such venting by operating a bypass valve or activating an emergency damper to relieve pressure in the system. A pressure build-up left unabated can cause a massive explosion that will destroy the boiler, wreak havoc on the surroundings, and kill or injure all those nearby.

Airships, Aeroplanes, and Other Vehicles

Airships consist of hulls or gondolas borne aloft by large silk-and-rubber gas-bags, thrust by steam-driven propellers, and steered by the manipulation of sails, rudders, and wings. The hazards of aerial travel adds to its charm: bad weather, mountainous terrain, mechanical difficulties, and—particularly along the wilder frontiers of civilized society—air pirates.

Aeroplanes are lightweight mechanical contrivances achieving sustained flight by some combination of wing-created lift and airscrew-powered propulsion. They are for local travel only, lacking the endurance for extended trips—though a small aeroplane might conceivably barnstorm across the country, landing in fields and sheltering in barns. However, this won't be much faster, if at all, than floating in luxurious elegance aboard an airship, and there is a real possibility of the firebox running out of fuel: a disastrous event, as it replenishes the boiler driving the airscrews or ornithopter wings or both.

Most airships carry at least one or two small aeroplanes for passenger excursions, cargo lading, and reconnoitering. Among the adventurous it is considered a sporting pastime to depart an airship by means of parachute to be retrieved by aeroplane.

Additionally, clanking steam-powered mechanical walkers called juggernauts are common in the east among nations under the influence of the Muscovite Empire. They are slow and affected by adverse terrain, but are more robust than delicate aerial machinery. Similarly, railroads do exist, but are mostly used for moving cargo and the less well-off.

Perform

This represents your skill at dramatic or musical performance, including oratorical declamation as well as singing, playing an instrument, acting, and reciting poetry with true and tender feeling.

 Overcome: This lets you deal with obstacles related to the difficulty of the material to be performed or of piercing the jaded ennui of the audience.

 Create an Advantage: A skillful performance can create a positive impression on members of the audience, or give you a reputation for taste and refinement.

 Attack: Perform is not typically used to attack.

 Defend: Perform is not typically used to defend.

Perform Stunts

Virtuoso: Choose a mode of performance. +2 to Perform when overcoming obstacles related to the difficulty of this type of material.

Pilot

This is your ability to steer and operate an aerial machine—including airships and aeroplanes—as well as to navigate by means of dead reckoning, map reading, and using a compass and sextant.

 Overcome: Deal with difficulties of maneuver and navigation, including attempting to come alongside another airship or dock an aeroplane with an airship.

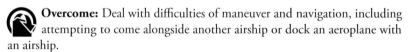 **Create an Advantage:** Pilot can create advantages related to aerial maneuvering.

 Attack: Pilot is not typically used to attack.

 Defend: Pilot is used to defend against attempts to shoot at or board your craft.

Pilot Stunts

Combat Pilot: You can use Pilot in place of Shoot to attack in air combat when flying an aeroplane.

Fancy Flying: +2 to Pilot when overcoming obstacles related to close-quarters maneuvering in an aeroplane, such as flying nap of the earth, threading among looming airships, or zig-zagging along a narrow valley.

Scholarship

This reflects your formal education, schooling, and book learning. It probably includes at least a smattering of classical languages as well as a grounding in literature, history, science, philosophy, and mathematics.

 Overcome: Scholarship can be used to remedy obstacles related to lack of knowledge or historical information.

 Create an Advantage: You can use Scholarship to create advantages related to knowing facts important to the situation or to applying the insights of scholarly observation and deduction. For example, while sightseeing or attending fairs and exhibitions, Scholarship can allow you to discern things that others might miss.

 Attack: Scholarship is not typically used to attack.

Defend: Scholarship is not typically used to defend.

Scholarship Stunts

Law Degree: Because of your legal training, you can use Scholarship to overcome obstacles and create advantages related to the invocation of legal machinery, including the action of courts and the law.

Medical Degree: You are a licensed physician, and can use Scholarship to overcome obstacles and create advantages related to the deployment of medical knowledge, including the diagnosis of disease and the skillful treatment of injury.

Society

This reflects your position in society and the extensiveness of your social circle. It includes the niceties of decorum and etiquette, as well as the knowledge of appropriate conventions for interacting within and across class boundaries. Using Society produces correct and cordial interrelations, but not the true intimacy and friendship that can emerge by engaging in honest, sincere, authentic conversation by using Converse. Note that Deceit, not Society, is generally used to pass as something you are not—for example, a commoner wishing to be thought of as high-born would use Deceit rather than Society to make his or her way among the aristocrats.

 Overcome: Use Society to gain introductions to those with whom you would like to become better acquainted, to smooth over minor gaffes and faux pas, and to otherwise lubricate social interaction.

Create an Advantage: Use Society to create advantages related to the favorable opinion of society's great and good, to your social connections and position, and to your ability to handle yourself correctly in polite society.

Attack: Society is used to "cut" your inferiors or snub your peers; those of higher status are generally immune to the jealous insubordination of the *hoi polloi*, so you can only use Society to attack someone of equal or lower social rank. Use your place in society aspect to judge this; if the answer isn't obvious, then the attack is permitted.

Defend: Society is not typically used to defend; use Will instead.

Society Stunts

A Wonderful Correspondent: Because of your extensive letter-writing, you have a far-flung network of friends and acquaintances. You can spend a fate point to introduce such an NPC into the scene where appropriate, or to declare that a newly introduced NPC is one of your correspondents.

Honored Stranger: Under normal circumstances, your foreign origin marks you as an outsider in Britannic society. However, you are treated as an honored guest by one circle, social group, or class—such as diplomats, artists, businessmen, musicians, or scientists. Among that group, you gain +2 Society.

EXTRA: VEHICLES

Permissions: An aspect indicating ownership, possession, or use of a vehicle.
Costs: Refresh

A vehicle is defined by its high concept, indicating the type of vehicle it is. It starts with 3 free stunts and 3 refresh. A vehicle's fate points are used by its crew, whether they are commanding from it, operating it, maintaining it, or fighting from it. The size of the vehicle determines its Hull skill and the number of boxes on its hull stress track. A vehicle has a Hull skill, used to prevent damage from attacks, determined by its size. A typical vehicle is normal size, giving it Fair (+2) Hull and 2 **hull stress boxes**, which indicate its ability to take damage. Its size can be changed by the Hull Size stunt. A vehicle's skills are determined by its crew, which is Mediocre (+0) in all things, but again can be changed by taking stunts, particularly Crew Training.

Vehicles attack using the Guns skill of its crew or, if a PC is handling the gunnery, his or her Shoot skill. In aerial combat, vehicles typically fire at each other using the crew's Guns skill while attempting to avoid the other vehicle's fire via adroit maneuvering using the crew's Pilot skill. Should an attack hit, the defending vehicle rolls Hull to overcome a passive difficulty equal to the shifts inflicted by the Guns attack. If the vehicle does not succeed, its player checks off a hull stress box with a value equal to or greater than the shifts inflicted by the attack. If a vehicle has no hull stress boxes that can absorb the hit, or when it loses its last hull stress box, it is taken out. Vehicles do not have consequence slots.

The size ladder for vehicles has the following levels: small, normal, large, huge, enormous, and gigantic. For each increment of size a vehicle possesses, it gets 1 hull stress box and 1 rank in Hull. For each increment of size difference between two vehicles, the smaller vehicle gets +1 to its crew's Pilot rolls to maneuver against the larger ship, while the larger ship gets +1 to its Hull rolls to withstand damage caused by the smaller ship's Guns. For example, a small fighter aeroplane going up against a gigantic aerial dreadnought would get +5 to its Pilot roll to outmaneuver the larger vessel, while the dreadnought would get +5 to its Hull roll against the fighter's Guns.

It may come to pass that the tiny Pension Bellevue finds itself with a gigantic aerial dreadnought bearing down upon it. The obvious course of action is flight! However, plucky passengers aboard the floating hostel may take it upon themselves to behave in true Britannic fashion and take up arms against the foe. It is unlikely that this will go well. GMs, if you wish to give the players a chance, let them invoke an appropriate aspect they have created as an advantage against the aerial dreadnought to cause an attack to be **armor-piercing**. An armor-piercing attack inflicts its shifts upon an enemy vehicle automatically, bypassing the Hull roll to overcome the damage.

Stunts for Airships, Aeroplanes, and Other Vehicles

Airworthy: The vehicle is particularly well-designed, giving +2 to its crew's Mechanics rolls to maintain, repair, or otherwise keep the vehicle flying.

Armed: The first time this stunt is taken, the vehicle can fire upon opposing craft using its crew's Guns skill or a PC's Shoot skill. Each additional time this stunt is taken, it increases the gunner's Guns or Shoot skill by one rank while manning the vehicle's guns.

Armored: The vehicle is particularly well-armored. Each time this stunt is taken, the ship gains one rank in Hull.

Crew Training: The vehicle's crew is particularly skilled, well-trained, or experienced. The crew's skill stack increases by one rank.

Distinctive: The vehicle gets an additional aspect. This stunt can be taken multiple times.

Fast: +2 to the crew's Pilot (or Drive) skills when chasing or being chased, or in other, similar circumstances where the speedier vessel would have a marked advantage.

Hull Size: Increase the vehicle's hull size by one—from normal to large, large to enormous, and enormous to gigantic. Alternately, decrease the vehicle's hull size from normal to small and gain one refresh. This stunt can be taken multiple times.

Nimble: +2 to the crew's Pilot (or Drive) rolls when dogfighting, maneuvering in tight quarters, or other circumstances where turning quickly and precisely would be advantageous.

Numerous: Rather than one vessel, there are many. Each time this stunt is taken, double the number of available craft—for example, taking this stunt the first time would double the number of vessels from one to two.

Sloppy Controls: The vehicle is hard to control, rendering it less maneuverable than similar vessels. -2 to the crew's Pilot (or Drive) rolls. The vessel gains one refresh.

Special Weapon: The vehicle has a special weapon—such as a ram, aerial harpoon, or gas projector. It could also be a device employed in a non-standard way or one that has non-standard effects, such as a ram that allows an airship to use its Hull to attack other airships, or an aerial harpoon that allows an airship to hamper an opposing ship's maneuverability, reducing the opposing crew's Pilot skill.

Pension Bellevue

The Pension Bellevue is an ***Elegant, Old-Fashioned Sky-Salon***. It is normal size—giving it Fair (+2) Hull and 2 hull stress boxes—and has 3 refresh. The players can choose its 3 free stunts and allocate its refresh to stunts as desired.

Air versus Ground

Airships and juggernauts are comparable in speed, although airships are not restricted by terrain in the same way as juggernauts. However, juggernauts can use terrain for cover and concealment, unlike airships. GMs, when airships face off against juggernauts, you may wish to allow airships the benefit of the Fast stunt and juggernauts the benefit of the Nimble stunt.

Aeroplanes, on the other hand, are much faster and more maneuverable than both juggernauts and airships. To reflect this, you may wish to give aeroplanes the benefit of the Fast and Nimble stunts when facing juggernauts, airships, or both. However, their range is much more limited, so you can give aeroplanes the aspect **Limited Fuel Capacity**, which can be compelled to force them to head back to base immediately, or to run an appreciable risk of crashing if they don't.

Strength in Numbers

Sometimes, many vehicles will swarm around another—for instance, if a squadron of sky-pirates assaults the Pension Bellevue—but you might not want to track each swarming craft. In that case, the swarming vehicles can attack *en masse*, giving them a combined attack roll with a bonus for each doubling of their numbers: +1 for 2–3 attackers, +2 for 4–7, +3 for 8–15, +4 for 16–31, and so forth. An attack against a group of swarming attackers is made once, but can affect each member individually.

For example, if a squadron of 8 sky pirates in small aeroplanes attacked the normal-sized Pension Bellevue in two groups of four planes each, each attack would get +2 versus the Pilot skill of the Pension Bellevue's crew, and the Pension Bellevue would get +1 to its Hull roll to overcome any shifts of damage because it is one rung higher on the size ladder. Assuming the PCs have armed their floating hotel, the Pension Bellevue would counterattack, rolling its crew's Guns or a PC's Shoot, opposed by the sky pirate's Pilot, which would get +1 because each is one rung lower on the size ladder. On a successful attack by the Pension Bellevue, each defending aeroplane rolls Hull to overcome passive opposition equal to the shifts inflicted by the sky-salon's gunners. Each aeroplane that failed this roll would lose its sole hull box.

Vehicle Examples

Muscovite Aeroplane Squadron

Crew Skills: Good (+3) Pilot, Fair (+2) Guns, Average (+1) Will

Stunts: Numerous ×2 (8 aeroplanes), Hull Size (small), Armed, Crew Training ×3 (+3 to skill stack)

Hull Size: Small (1 hull stress box, Average Hull, +1 refresh)

Hull Skill: Average (+1)

Hull Stress: ☐

Refresh: 0

Venetian Floating Sky-Palace

Distinctive Aspects: *Tethered in Place*, *Awash in Elegance*

Stunts: Hull Size ×4 (gigantic), Distinctive ×2 (2 distinctive aspects)

Hull Size: Gigantic (5 hull stress boxes, Superb Hull)

Hull Skill: Superb (+5)

Hull Stress: ☐☐☐☐☐

Refresh: 0

Britannic Aerial Patrol Ship

Crew Skills: Great (+4) Will, Good (+3) Guns, Fair (+2) Pilot, Average (+1) Mechanics

Stunts: Hull Size (large), Armed, Crew Training ×4 (+4 to skill stack)

Hull Size: Large (3 hull stress boxes, Good Hull)

Hull Skill: Good (+3)

Hull Stress: ☐☐☐

Refresh: 0

Barbary Sky-Pirate Ship

Crew Skills: Good (+3) Pilot, Fair (+2) Guns, Average (+1) Mechanics

Stunts: Armed, Fast, Crew Training ×3 (+3 to skill stack)

Hull Size: Normal (2 hull stress boxes, Fair Hull)

Hull Skill: Fair (+2)

Hull Stress: ☐☐

Refresh: 1

Muscovite Juggernaut

Crew Skills: Good (+3) Guns, Fair (+2) Drive, Average (+1) Mechanics

Stunts: Armed, Armored (+1 Hull rank), Crew Training ×3 (+3 to skill stack)

Hull Size: Normal (2 hull stress boxes, Fair Hull)

Hull Skill: Good (+3)

Hull Stress: ☐☐

Refresh: 1

RUNNING THE ADVENTURE

Once the PCs have been created, begin the game with them aboard the Pension Bellevue as it is about to cast off its moorings. By default, the game begins in Paris, but you can choose a different city—one closer to the action that emerged in the Great Power game, for example—if that seems appropriate. Have the players introduce their characters by interacting with NPCs or other PCs; they may be standing at the balustrade, waving to well-wishers below, or occupying themselves with whatever other activities they wish.

Introduce one or two NPCs, foreshadowing their significance. For example, in **The Aerial Heiress**, if Mademoiselle Chandru or Ambassador Dunkelfeld or analogous characters are not PCs, now is a good time to make their presence known. Dunkelfeld will have bodyguards with him, square-jawed and humorless Prussian military men in plainclothes. Mme. Chandru will be terribly mysterious and exotic. Your NPCs should promise to complement or augment the PC's stories rather than threaten to suck all the air out of the room, narratively speaking.

After introducing these NPCs, the Pension Bellevue begins its journey. Have the first and each subsequent aerial leg of the journey reflect the backstories of the PCs. Each leg of the trip encompasses one round of actions from the PCs and appropriate NPCs; usually this will take the form of interaction among characters, but there may be sneaking around and skulduggery, especially as the action heats up. This is a good time to look at the PCs' aspects and compel them ruthlessly.

At each new destination, do two things: First, make the PCs feel like they're traveling. Use the location aspects to suggest events and excursions—opportunities for the PCs to show off their athletic prowess, cultural *savoir faire*, or other fine qualities. You may wish to introduce an NPC who wants something from, or can offer something to, a PC.

Second, develop the grand strategic situation and connect it to what's going on aboard the ship, as discussed above. If the players like, when the Pension Bellevue arrives at a new location, play out a turn of the Great Power game, where appropriate; any aspects created can then feed into in the character-level game.

For example, in **The Aerial Heiress**, the PCs will gradually learn that Ambassador Dunkelfeld seems to want something from Mme. Chandru, something she is reluctant to give him. Here, aspects relating to gallantry are ripe for compels. Over time, the PCs may discover that Dunkelfeld is trying to arrange a marriage between the Azeri heiress and a Prussian nobleman with strong ties to the Muscovite royal family. This marriage will bring an important Caucasian fueling stop under the control of Muscovy, posing a threat to Britannia's Bactrian possessions. Patriotic PCs will be aghast at the threat; others will see opportunities. For her part, Mme. Chandru is a modern woman and refuses to wed a man she does not love. She may find a PC appealing, or there may be a dashing sheikh from the court of the Caliph who has already won her heart—or perhaps he is traveling incognito in order to woo her, and needs the PCs' help. If the PCs don't intervene, Dunkelfeld will work his wiles upon the young woman, and she will feel duty-bound to go through with the marriage; perhaps her father or her beau will be targeted for retaliation if she doesn't? But if this or something like it happens, an emboldened Muscovite autocrat will feel empowered to push further than he normally would in an ongoing diplomatic imbroglio, and thus through miscalculation recklessly hurl the continent into all-out war.

For example, if the Caliphate and Britannia have signed some sort of mutual assistance treaty in the Great Power game, the prospect of the marriage will give the Tsar a pretext to send some of his juggernaut forces into the Caucasus—as an honor guard for the wedding, perhaps. But this will incense the Caliph, who will step up security on the border, creating the possibility of a provocation, manufactured or otherwise, that results in Britannia's being called upon to redeem its treaty obligations, potentially causing a much wider war.

Convey this danger somehow to the PCs. If all else fails, deliver the relevant geopolitical developments by employing a Britannic boffin, savvy in international politics and traveling aboard the Pension Bellevue. If the PCs can forestall the danger by preventing a successful Prussian courtship, so much the better. If not, ratchet up the international tension and have the PCs beset by historical circumstances trending toward war: tighter border controls, a stronger and more trigger-happy military presence, news of mobilizations and deployments, and so forth.

In **Spy in the Sky**, the spy will make cautious attempts to purloin documents relevant to her mission, using other characters as catspaws in the process, hoping to keep suspicion away from herself. Though she hopes to accomplish her mission by stealth, something will inevitably go wrong and the PCs will be on to her. Luckily, her accomplices will swoop in for a rendezvous and rescue if she can signal them. If she escapes or passes off her documents, the PCs may be the only ones in a position to interfere and prevent Britannia's secrets from falling into the hands of her enemies.

In **The Soft Crusade**, the PCs will eventually notice that the departure of the Pension Bellevue from a particular location means that it will soon be visited by violence and demonstrations in the street, since the *agent provocateur* aboard the sky-salon is operating under strict orders that give no leeway for hiding his tracks. As the reports of civil disturbance catch up with the PCs, they might begin to investigate, keeping their eyes open for suspicious behavior among their fellows aboard the ship. However, they will certainly become interested when a Britannic special agent, zealous but not particularly sharp, arrives with orders to apprehend the provocateur—and takes one of the PCs as his prime suspect!

Meanwhile, the guilty party will be making contact with the Pope's agents and sympathizers on the ground, setting into motions acts of sabotage and violence, causing disturbances, and spreading rumors and innuendo against the secular authorities, who may crack down on the perpetrators, but in so doing ratchet up the diplomatic tension even further.

COUNTDOWN TO WAR

Developments in the international situation will have consequences for those on the Pension Bellevue. Each level of development ratchets up the diplomatic tension, which can be used as passive opposition against attempts to cross borders and to avoid official interference. It will also complicate smuggling of contraband goods and other international crimes. Increase the tension whenever events warrant it, or at the end of each leg of the journey.

- Alarming Headlines (Average [+1] Diplomatic Tension)

- Diplomatic Protestations (Fair [+2] Diplomatic Tension)

- Popular Demonstrations (Good [+3] Diplomatic Tension)

- A Shooting Incident along the Frontier (Great [+4] Diplomatic Tension)

- Full-Scale Mobilization (Superb [+5] Diplomatic Tension)

- Declaration of War! (Fantastic [+6] Diplomatic Tension)

FATE: WORLDS OF ADVENTURE

THE JOURNEY

Using the Map

The game map consists of nodes, representing important or interesting cities, and links, each representing several days of travel by airship. Travel times can be reduced by using Pilot or Mechanics to overcome the distance, but the minimum time is about a day per link. This map isn't fixed; if it misses some of your favorite locations, replace an existing node or add a new one and connect it as desired.

Events in the Air

For each leg of the trip, roll three fate dice and consult the table below to determine if anything interesting happens while traveling. To read the table, start at the top-left corner. For each ⊞, go right one cell; for each ⊟, go down one cell. So, a roll of ⊞⊟⊞—equivalent to ⊞⊞⊟ or ⊟⊞⊞—results in Storms Ahead.

Add the result as an aspect to the scene with a free invocation. GMs, you control this aspect, but the PCs can use it to makes things more interesting by compelling NPCs. The PCs can interact with each other and with NPCs as they wish—while lounging on deck, dining at a formal event with the captain, standing at the rail observing the scenery, entertaining each other in the salon, dancing in the ballroom, and so forth. If nothing of note seems likely to transpire, pass on quickly to the next destination after allowing a little time for roleplaying and planning for the upcoming stop.

Roll	⬜	⊞	⊞	⊞
⬛	Tempers Flare!	Crew Problems	Passenger Complaints	Airship Sighted!
⊟	What's That Noise?	Smooth Sailing	Storms Ahead	
⊟	Visibility Zero	Mechanical Trouble!		
⊟	Buzzed by Aeroplanes			

If the Pension Bellevue begins to crash, take this opportunity to introduce moments of high adventure and drama! Desperate action to survive the crash and its aftermath is the order of the day; give the PCs opportunities for heroics and poltroonery in equal measure. Survival is certainly possible if the vessel hits the ground—there are "lifeboats," of course, gliders and parachutes for those who act quickly enough. However, those still on board when the ship strikes will have to work hard to avoid taking consequences from the impact. Once the Pension Bellevue crashes, you can continue the game, but it might be time to end the game and have the players suggest epilogues for their characters.

Excursions on the Ground

When the Pension Bellevue arrives at a new destination, present the PCs with two or three opportunities for tourist excursions on the ground. You don't need to connect all of them to the plot, but try to link some of them. In some cases, you may need to assign passive opposition to a character's action as a tourist. Determine this randomly by rolling two fate dice and adding two to the result, giving results from Mediocre (+0) to Great (+4).

Sightseeing: Wandering around to glimpse the scenic and picturesque local attractions may serve merely as background color. Depending on the plot, though, it may give the PCs a chance to pick up useful and interesting things with Notice. If it is not immediately apparent what a PC might notice, roll three fate dice and consult the following table. Introduce the result as an aspect that you can invoke, or use it as a prompt in conjunction with the city description to initiate a colorful incident or curious episode.

Roll	◼	➕	➕	➕
◼	Trouble in the Streets	A Charming Local Guide	A Strange Coincidence	The Truly Sublime
➖	Curious Behavior	A Lovely Scene	Pushing and Shoving	
➖	Potential for Violence	We're Being Watched		
➖	Larceny in Progress			

If a PC notices something truly sublime—ancient or natural wonders, or moments of great emotional poignancy, for example—you could refresh all or part of their fate pool; similarly, seeing a lovely scene may deserve a reward of a single fate point. Notice that this subverts the normal fate point economy, which rewards players for their characters getting in trouble. If you wish, you might instead give the player a free invocation of the sublime or lovely aspect, or let the presence of such an aspect be its own reward. Still, the possibility of such a reward may further motivate the PCs to go to places where they can get in trouble.

Other events might create a situation aspect or be used to justify narrative complications. Failure to notice the noteworthy should result in a disadvantageous or otherwise unpleasant surprise, usually antagonistic attention from the locals, who may resent tourists or the airborne more generally—you can represent this with an aspect as well, which you can invoke once for free against the PCs.

Shopping: Excellent bargains and cheap souvenirs may be the fruit of shopping while in foreign lands; a PC can use Business to determine their success. Tourists who flash their wealth might attract unwanted attention from local pickpockets, burglars, and thugs, while indiscriminate shoppers might gain a reputation among their traveling companions for execrable taste.

Hunting and Fishing: Depending on the circumstances, hunting could take the form of wandering through wood and field with rifle in hand (Shoot), chasing hounds on horseback (Athletics) in pursuit of a fox, or even following a hawk in an aeroplane (Pilot) as it takes geese, ducks, and other fowl in the air.

Parties, Balls, and Galas: Convivial occasions are a chance to mix with companions and newfound acquaintances (Converse, Deceive, Provoke). Use Society to make appropriate connections based on your place in society aspect; making connections across class lines is more difficult (Good to Superb), but some affairs such as masquerades and carnivals are notorious for blurring or inverting class distinctions. The PCs may be called upon to perform at small, informal gatherings (Perform); at large balls and galas the younger folk are inclined to dance (Athletics). Success at such endeavors may impress new acquaintances, and romantic entanglements may transpire as a result. If desired, a character can defend against falling in love with Will or Society.

Fairs and Exhibitions: Local organizations and communities often come together to display and celebrate their unique products, offerings, and talents—whether agricultural, cultural, or professional. Use Notice as with sightseeing above, but there are different things to see. Friends from home might be familiar faces or countrymen newly met on foreign soil; a brush with greatness is a passing encounter with a notable NPC personage, perhaps an alternate version of some familiar real-world historical figure.

Roll	■	✚	✚	✚
■	Noisy Protests	Brush with Greatness	Friends from Home	The Truly Marvelous
⊟	Curious Behavior	An Impressive Demonstration	It's For Sale!	
⊟	A Ludicrous Display	A Local Curiosity		
⊟	It's Out of Control!			

Sports: Athletic entertainment such as golf, football, and archery may be arranged formally or informally, with tourists invited to participate. Successful participation may gain you new friends or the beginnings of a local reputation. Additionally, the honor of Britannia may be at stake!

Betting and Gambling: Here is where the Gamble skill comes into its own. On the ground, at casinos and betting parlors, roll Gamble against passive opposition based on the quality of the house in order to make money—in other words, to create a financial stress box of the appropriate value. Failing terribly, such as a Poor (-1) showing, may result in the character owing money to certain unsavory types. This can be represented by a negative aspect reflecting the disapprobative and censorious attention of some captain of the criminal *demi-monde*, such as *Legbreakers on His Tail*.

Gazetteer

Use the information that follows for quick descriptions of the regions through which the PCs pass. Extrapolate this information expansively to create plot hooks and NPCs with whom to entangle the characters. Augment or change these aspects to align them with the features of interest or importance to the PCs.

Alexandria

This ancient city on the Mediterranean coast near the mouth of the Nile is a Britannic protectorate, *a transit point for cargo* to be unloaded from maritime vessels and laden aboard airships headed for India and China; Egyptian cotton is a principal export for ships headed to Britannic factories. There are *many commercial opportunities here* ripe for the plucking, although the expatriate local representatives—called factors—of the *Britannic North African Company* are jealous of their prerogatives and may try to cut out an interloper. Tourists may enjoy the local ruins or *sightseeing along the Nile*.

Algiers

This picturesque city sits on a hill sloping down toward the sea. It is the *headquarters of the Britannic Foreign Legion*, which issues commands from the citadel called the Casbah that sits above *a labyrinthine warren of whitewashed walls*. There is a large European community here, including *many dissolute Provencal aristocrats* seeking to restore their fortunes by investing in highly speculative real-estate deals and other commercial ventures aimed at opening up the North African interior. Nearby *seaside resorts* provide opportunities for swimming and being admired for one's physical beauty as well as for hobnobbing with the fashionable crowd.

Athens

The ruins of this ancient city—cradle of Britannic and indeed all Western civilization, and once home to the philosophers Socrates, Plato, and Aristotle—are fascinating to those with an appreciation of history or an education in the classics. *The famous Parthenon* surmounts the Acropolis that rises proudly over the city, which is otherwise *a backwater province* ruled over by an *officious and corrupt officer of the Caliphate* who turns a blind eye and a grasping palm toward the smuggling of antiquities from the region.

In case of hostilities or other unpleasantness with the Caliphate, Britannic airships may bypass Athens to refuel and refurbish at the Britannic outpost on Crete, where there is a strong military presence centered around the *harbor-fortress of Heraklion*.

Belgrade

Belgrade currently marks the northern extent of the Caliphate's possessions within Europe. Its governor bears the exalted rank of *pasha*, and his standard flies three horse-tails to convey his immense dignity. Over the past several centuries, the city has been ***traded back and forth*** in the border conflicts between the Caliphate and the now very much-shrunken Holy Roman Empire, an independent kingdom with its current capital at Vienna. Belgrade bears the imprint of this history with ***an eclectic mix of Eastern and Western architectural forms***, giving the city ***an eccentric and romantic charm***. An active ***Serbian nationalist movement*** seeks to oust the Pasha and his Turkish soldiers from the region and has a strong presence in the agrarian hinterlands.

Berlin

This is the capital of Prussia, a ***Muscovite client state*** possessed of a ***strong army*** and a ***long-standing martial tradition*** that has frequently come into conflict with the Holy Roman Empire. The Prussians have ***borrowed Muscovite juggernaut technology***, and with their ***well-known efficiency*** they are reputed to have made several innovations about which the Britannic High Command would be very interested in learning more. Berlin itself boasts a ***risqué and exciting nightlife*** that rivals Paris in its energy and innovation, fueled by alcohol and other intoxicants—all rather shocking to Britannic sensibilities!

Budapest

Located **on the banks of the Danube**, Budapest is **one of the most beautiful cities in Europe**, and its numerous hot springs form the basis of **spas and baths** that attract many travelers. The city is the capital of the small, independent, **neutral Kingdom of Hungary** that emerged from the widespread unrest during the middle of the 19th century.

Florence

This city is the capital of the Grand Duchy of Tuscany, a **Britannic client state** in the northern part of the Italian peninsula. Its **museums and art galleries** reflect its long association with the arts and sciences, as "birthplace of the Renaissance" and home of Leonardo da Vinci; today, it is an important European **center of fashion** in dress and jewelry. Among the local bourgeoisie, **a movement to modernize** and revitalize the city's architecture has gained considerable sway, but Britannic interests resist this; they do not wish the city's antique charm to be damaged or lost.

Gibraltar

The Rock of Gibraltar is **a Britannic fortress**, impregnable and well-armed, with dreadnoughts moored to tethering pylons on the heights of the Rock itself above well-protected casemates **bristling with guns. Surrounded by the Sultanate of Andalusia**, the westernmost province of the Caliphate, Gibraltar is an important military base, and can withstand a siege almost indefinitely so long as it can be resupplied by sea or air. The commander of the garrison, a high-ranking Britannic general, is suspicious of strangers and the possibility of spying, infiltration, and sabotage, but the officers' wives—including his own—are **desperate for novelty**.

Istanbul

This city, once capital of the Eastern Roman Empire—or Byzantine Empire—is now one of the chief cities of the powerful Caliphate of Baghdad. The Sultan of Istanbul is known to be ambitious and eager for notice and promotion, and the primacy of the city, the seat of his power, is a considerable bolster to his ambitions. The grandeur of the **many historical palaces and mosques** that grace the city add to the appeal of Istanbul. It is still **an important crossroads** for land, sea, and now air travel. The mighty guns of the Caliphate—huge mortars, bombards, and cannons entrenched in strongly fortified bunkers guarding the landward and seaward approaches to the city—make Istanbul a **bastion of the Caliphate**.

Jerusalem

This is the *capital of Outremer*, the storied Christian kingdom of the East, now *a Britannic possession* whose regent rules in the name of the Queen. The aristocracy of Outremer are *a strange mix of East and West*, with Britannic language and manners but a fierce and cunning ruthlessness, which comes from centuries of being the elite minority charged with keeping order upon a fractious and *volatile populace* of mixed religious, ethnic, and political loyalties. The *Cardinal of Jerusalem* is one of the senior ecclesiastical authorities in Europe since the flight of the Pope to the Western hemisphere and the establishment of Novo Vaticano amid the coastal mountains of Huy Brasil in Papal America. Jerusalem's Biblical connections and historical significance make it a popular pilgrimage site.

London

This is the *capital of Britannia*, although it shares some of the administrative functions of governance with its sister city, Paris. A high-speed aerial courier service connects the two cities (+2 to rolls to travel between them quickly); it is used by important ministers and other officials, as well as by those who, by hook or by crook, manage to finagle a place aboard. There are those who consider London, with its *notorious fog* and its *stuffy overall Englishness*, to be the less favored conurbation of the pair, but it remains the great financial, social, scientific, and cultural *center of the Britannic nation*, truly an imperial capital.

Madrid

This is the chief city of the politically fragmented Iberian Peninsula. Madrid is nominally under the dominion of the Grand Duchy of La Mancha in the center of the region but is in effect *an open city*; to the north, the Kingdom of Léon and Castile is a Britannic client state concerned about its Portuguese and Andalusian rivals. Lisbon, the nearby capital of Catholic Portugal, is a popular port of embarkation for Novo Vaticano and points beyond in Papal America, and many travelers pass through Madrid en route to the New World. The city itself is a *cultural oasis*, with a *highly renowned opera company*, and *many highly trained artisans* who produce rare works of exquisite craftsmanship and incalculable value.

Marseilles

This is the chief Britannic city on the Mediterranean Sea, making it a *bustling aerial and maritime port*, located along a rugged coastal area whose numerous coves and inlets still permit a *vigorous smuggling trade* in illicit and contraband goods. Nearby, the Cote d'Azur—or French Riviera as it is often known—serves as a health resort and vacation site for many of the Britannic upper class; *many aerial yachts* are housed here in *exclusive air-marinas and sky-clubs*. The region is known for its *golf courses*, as well as the *high-class casinos* of the small independent principality of Monaco.

Munich

This is the capital of the Kingdom of Bavaria and one of the chief cities of central Europe, located on the banks of the Isar River north of the Bavarian Alps. It is *an industrial powerhouse* with a reputation for producing high-quality manufactured goods, although its workers are said to be *sticklers for rules and procedures*. In general, life proceeds at an easy pace throughout Bavaria, although the political leadership must keep an eye on its ambitious neighbors to the north, east, and, south.

Naples

The southern part of the Italian peninsula is nominally *an independent kingdom*, although the increasingly close ties of the Republic of Italy to the north with Britannia make the Kingdom of Naples susceptible to the influence of the Caliphate of Baghdad, particularly with nearby Sicily under the Caliph's sway. The Kingdom of Naples is home to a *large Catholic population*, even with the flight of the Papacy to the Western Hemisphere, and the city of Naples has *many churches and monasteries*. Its location near Mount Vesuvius and the ruins of Pompeii contribute to its scenic value, and it boasts lively trade as a result of its strategic location at the crossroads of the Mediterranean.

Nicosia

The Mediterranean isle of Cyprus, with its sunny slopes covered in olive groves and sheep pastures, is a *Britannic protectorate* governed by a High Commissioner, although the local mayor also holds considerable power. The town of Nicosia is *a sleepy backwater* with a mixed population of Turks, Greeks, Armenians, and "Latins" from the nearby Kingdom of Jerusalem, filled with *private gardens and public aqueducts*, all behind city walls built by the Venetian princes who once ruled here. A *museum of antiquities* proudly displays artifacts discovered on the island, some dating back to the days of ancient Greece.

Paris

This is one of the chief cities of Britannia, *a sprawling conurbation* extending along and out from the banks of the Seine. *Huge towers of ironwork lattice* reach gracefully skyward, serving as mooring points for the *many airships* that make Paris their home port or a major port of call. The ribaldry of its nightlife is legendary, and the *Bohemian quarters* of the city are a haven for artistry and experimentation. The working people of the city are known to harbor *radical sentiments* and on occasion noisily give vent to republican and anti-clerical opinions.

Prague

This city lies in the heart of Bohemia, one of the few remaining regions still under Habsburg rule. A *large student population* attending Charles University—founded by the eponymous Holy Roman Emperor in 1347, and now the oldest university in central Europe—gives certain precincts of the city an *energetic and youthful ambiance*. The current Prince of Bohemia, a young scion of the Habsburgs, lives in *Prague Castle*, where his court is well known for entertaining scientists, musicians, and artists—as well as charlatans such as astrologers, soothsayers, and magicians. But Prague is also a *bustling industrial center*, with busy factories supplied by the coal mines and ironworks of the surrounding region.

Rome

An ancient and storied city, once the center of the Western world, today Rome is the capital of the *Republic of Italy*, a Britannic client state. It is filled with *architectural wonders and historical monuments*; of particular interest to Britannic tourists are the sites where Lord Wellington's army fought with Pope Napoleon's forces during the Battle of Rome, prompting the famed Flight of the Papacy to what is now called Papal America. Skulduggery by Catholic revanchists and secular anti-clericals is a popular theme in Britannic "penny dreadfuls" aimed at the ignorant masses.

Strasbourg

This city is the capital of the principality of Alsace, a small but strategic Britannic client state along the west bank of the Rhine River. It is *charmingly provincial*, with its *Gothic architecture* redolent of the town's medieval origins. The famous *Strasbourg Cathedral* is a notable landmark, and the square in front of the old church is often filled with artists attempting to sketch its complex and intricate architectural lines.

Tunis

With a *well-protected harbor* in a lagoon called the Lake of Tunis surrounded by low limestone hills, Tunis is an *important naval base of the Caliphate* and boasts impressive *coastal and aerial defense artillery batteries* in great number. The city itself is picturesque, with *elegant minarets* towering over a *medina filled with shops and restaurants* located on an isthmus between the Lake of Tunis and Lake Sejoumi, and the *palace of the Emir of Tunis* is an architectural marvel.

Venice

The *cloud-city* of Venice is notable for its *balloon-borne palaces*, floating in the air above the *drowned ruins* of old Venice and anchored in place by thick cables of twisted copper sheathed in silk. Its ancient noble families host *masquerades of exquisite whimsy and dream-like romance*, where masked dancers turn out on open-air pavilions looking out upon the world below. Many of the great artworks and artifacts of previous eras are displayed here in the *private collections* of the Venetian nobility.

Vienna

A center of modernist high culture, this city is the administrative center of the Habsburg monarchy and the Holy Roman Empire. Its *coffeehouses* are rife with political, artistic, and philosophical talk. Exciting work in the *new field of psychoanalysis* is conducted and discussed here, and it hosts an *avant-garde* school of musical composers known for their eerie and startling atonality.

Warsaw

The former Grand Duchy of Warsaw is under the *dominion of the Muscovite Empire*, and its mayor is a Russian-born appointee of the Tsar. He is active in his efforts to improve the civil infrastructure of the city, and there is *much construction* going on in the city at the moment, including the paving of roads, laying of pipes, and installation of street lighting, ably overseen by a Britannic expatriate.

Ending the Adventure

End the adventure when the PCs' ambitions have either been fulfilled or frustrated permanently, or when the general conflagration moots their individual desires. There are a couple of ways to wrap things up. You could go around the table and let the players suggest their character's fate in the context of how things turned out—war or peace, success or failure, and so forth. Or—if it came to war—you could zoom back out to the Great Power level and fight out this Europe's Great War, letting the PCs be killed as a mild consequence to the Great Power to which they had declared loyalty. Alternately, if the PCs somehow managed to avert or delay the war, and there is sufficient interest in continuing the game, simply pick up the adventure at a convenient point—perhaps when the Pension Bellevue once again prepares to depart Paris for a *romance dans l'air!*

This adventure was made awesome thanks to our Patreon patrons at patreon.com/evilhat—thanks guys!

INSIDERS

Alan Bartholet
Alexander Gräfe
Alexander R. Corbett
Amethyst Lynx
Andrew Sier
Anne-Sylvie Betsch
Antero Garcia
Arlo B Evans
ArthurDent
Brandon Burger
Brett Abbott
brian allred
Brian Chase
C. J. Hunter
C.K. Lee
Cerity
Charlton Wilbur
Chris Caporaso
Christian
Christian Svalander

Christopher Gunning
Dan Moody
Daniel
Daniel Gallant
Daniel Linder Krauklis
David
David Dorward
David E Ferrell
David L Kinney
David Reed
Donald Wheeler
Dustin Evermore
Eden Brandeis
Edgardo A Montes
Rosa
Edward MacGregor
Elsidar Amhransidhe
Emmanuel
eneko zarauz
Eric Bontz

Eric Willisson
Ezekiel Norton
Frank
Frédéri POCHARD
Gavran
Glenn Mochon
Graham
Graham Wills
Gregory Hirsch
Griffin Mitchell
Haakon Thunestvedt
Harry Lewis
Heron Jay Adkins
Jack Stephenson-Carr
Jacob Moffitt
James F Thunberg
Jason
Jason Blalock
Jason Cotton
Jason F Broadley

Jason Tocci
Jean-Christophe
Cubertafon
Jeff Craig
Jeff Xilon
Jere Krischel
Jeremiah McCoy
Jeremy DeVore
Jeremy Tidwell
Jim Nicholson
Jin Shei
Johannes K.
Rasmussen
John Beattie
John Rogers
John Rudd
John Wyatt
Jon
Jon-Pierre Gentil
Jordan Dennis

José Luis Porfirio
Joshua Reubens
Juanma Barranquero
Katie Ramsey
Keith Stanley
Ken
Ken Ditto
Kenji Ikiryo
Kevin Li
Larry Hollis
Leif Erik Furmyr
LeSquide
Marc Mundet
Mark Miller
Marshall Smith
Marty Chodorek
Matt and Nykki
Boersma
Matt Anderson
Matthew Broome

Matthew Dickson
Matthew Orwig
Matthew Whiteacre
Micah Davis
Michael Bowman
Michael Green
Michael Shumate
Morgan Ellis
Nick
Nick Bate
Nick Reale
Nicola Urbinati
Nicolas Marjanovic
Osye Pritchett
Pablo Martínez
Merino
Patrick Ewing
Patrick Mueller-Best
Paul Shawley

Paulo Rafael
Guariglia
Escanhoela
Pavel Zhukov
peter burczyk
Peter Gates
Peter Hatch
Philip Nicholls
PK
Randy Oest
Richard Bellingham
Rick
Rick Jakins
Riggah
Robert Hanz
Robert Kemp
Rod Meek
Roger Edge
Ryan
Ryan Singer

Sanchit
Sarah Vakos
Scott Hamilton
Sean
Sean Smith
Selene O'Rourke
Sharif Abed
Shervyn von Hoerl
Stephen Rider
Tim L Nutting
Timothy Carroll
Troy Ray
Will Goring
William J. White
William Lee
William McDuff
Woodrow Jarvis Hill
Zach

ADVENTURERS

Adam Gutschenritter
Aidan Grey
Alan Phillips
Alex Norris
Alexander
Alexander Permann
Alexey Kreshchuk
Alexis Lee
Allan Bray
Andrew Betts
Andrew Dacey
Andrew Grant
Andrew Lloyd
Andrew Loch
Andrew Turbott
Andy Arminio
Angus MacDonald
Anthony Popowski
Antoine Pempie
Arlene Medder
Arne Babenhauserheide
Asier Serras
athalbert
Augustus Vaitkevičius
Austin Stanley
Aviv
B. Bredthauer
Barac Wiley
beket
Ben Howard
Benjamin Welke
Bill
Björn Steffen
Blake Hutchins
Bo Bertelsen
Brad Davies
Brandon Metcalf
Brandon Wiley
Brandt
Brendan Conway
Brent Ritch
Brett Ritter
Brian Batchelder
Brian Bentley
Brian Creswick
Brian Koehler
Brian Kurtz
Brian S. Holt
Bruno Pereira
Bryan
Bryan Gillispie
Bryan Hilburn
Bryce
Bryce Perry
Caleb Figgers
Carl McLaughlin
Carl-William
Carlos Martin
Charles Chapman
Charles Kirk
Charlie Vick
Chip Dunning
Chris & Brigid Hirst
Chris Edwards

Chris Heilman
Chris Kurts
Chris Lock
Chris Mitchell
Chris Nolen
Chris Turner
Christian Lajoie
Christoph Thill
Christopher Allen
Christopher Avery
Christopher Smith Adair
Christopher W. Dolunt
Chuck
Cody Marbach
Cole Busse
Colin
Colin Matter
Craig Andera
Craig Mason
Craig Wright
Curt Meyer
Cyrano Jones
Dain
Dan Behlings
Dan Hall
Daniel Chapman
daniel hagglund
Daniel Hernández
Daniel Kraemer
Daniel Ley
Daniel Markwig
Daniel P. Espinosa
Daniel Roe
Daniel Ross
Daniel Taylor
Darren Lute
Dave
David
David
David Bellinger
David Bowers
David Buswell-Wible
David Goodwin
David Maple
David Millians
David Morrison
David Olson
David Rezak
David Silberstein
David Stern
Davide Orlandi
Declan Feeney
Denis Ryan
Derek Mayne
Dianne
Didier Bretin
Dillard
Don Arnold
Doug Blakeslee
Douglas
Doyce Testerman
Drew Shiel
Duncan
Dylan Sinnott

Earl Butler
Ebenezer Arvigenius
Eirch Mascariatu
Elsa S. Henry
Eric I
Eric Poulton
Eric Steen
Erik Ottosen
Ernie Sawyer
Etienne Olieu
Evan Jorgenson
Fabrice Breau
FelTK
Florent Poulpy Cadio
Florian Greß
Francis Dickinson
Frank Beaver
Frank G. Pitt
Frank Jarome
Frédérick Périgord
Gabriel Whitehead
Galen Pejeau
Garrett
Garrett Jones
Gary Anastasio
Gavin
Genevieve
Geoff
Geoffrey
Gian Domenico Facchini
Glynn Stewart
Gonzalo Dafonte Garcia
Graham Meinert
Greg Park
Gregg Workman
Gregory Fisher
Gustavo Campanelli
Heather
Henry Brown
Herman Duyker
HFB
Hillary Brannon
Howard M Thompson
Huston Todd
Ian Charlton
Ian Noble
Ian Stanley
Indi Latrani
Irene Strauss
Isaac Carroll
Ismael
Ivan Begley
J. Brandon Massengill
Jack Gulick
Jackson Hsieh
Jaime Robertson
Jake Linford
James
James Boldock
James Crowell
James Heide
James Husum
James Rouse
James Schultz

James Stuart
James Winfield
Jamie Wheeler
Jan Stals
Janet
Jared Hunt
Jason
Jason Bean
Jason Best
Jason Lee Waltman
Jason Lund
Jason Mill
Jason Pasch
Javier Gaspoz
Jayna Pavlin
Jean-François Robillard
Jeffrey Boman
Jeffrey Collyer
Jens
Jens Alfke
Jeremy Glick
Jeremy Hamaker
Jeremy Kear
Jeremy Kostiew
Jeremy Wong
jerry anning
Jesse
JF Paradis
Joanna
Joe
Joe Patterson
Joe.D
Joel Beebe
John
John Bogart
John Buczek
John Clayton
John Fiala
John Hawkins
John Hildebrand
John Lambert
John Petritis
John Portley
John Taber
John Tobin
John William McDonald
Johnathan Wright
Jon Rosebaugh
Jon Smejkal
Jonas Matser
Jonas Richter
Jonathan
Jonathan
Jonathan Dietrich
Jonathan Finke
Jonathan Hobbs
Jonathan Korman
Jonathan Rose
Joonas Iivonen
Jordan Deal
Jose A.
Joseph Formoso
Josh Rensch
Joshua

Joshua
Joshua Ramsey
JP
Juan Francisco Gutierrez
Julianna Backer
Julien Delabre
Jürgen Rudolph
Justin
Justin Beeh
Justin Thomason
Kaarchin
Karl Naylor
Keith Byrd
Kenny Norris
Kenny Snow
Kevin Flynn
Kevin Lindgren
Kevin McDermott
Kevin Payne
Kevin Veale
Kieren Martin
Krista
Kurt Zdanio
Kyle
Lanarch
Lars Ericson
Lester Ward
Link Hughes
Lisa Hartjes
Lisa M
Lobo
Loren Norman
Louie Perez
Lowell Francis
Luca Agosto
Lucas Bell
Lucian Smith
Ludo Bermejo
Lukar
M Kenny
M. Alan Thomas II
m.h.
Manfred
Marc
Marc Kevin Hall
Marcel Lotz
Marcel Wittram
Marcus
Mario Dongu
Marius Seebach
Mark
Mark A. Schmidt
Mark Gedak
Mark Harris
Mark Widner
Markus Haberstock
Markus Schoenlau
Marley Griffin
Martin Deppe
Mason
Masque Raccoon
Mathias Exner
Matt Clay
Matthew Karabache

Matthew Miller
Matthew Whalley
Matti Rintala
Maurice Strubel
Max
Max Kaehn
Michael
Michael
Michael
Michael Barrett
Michael D. Blanchard
Michael D. Ranalli Jr.
Michael Hill
Michael Hopcroft
Michael McCully
Michael Thompson
Mighty Meep
Mike de Jong
Mike Vermont
Misdirected Mark Productions
Naomi McArthur
Nathan Barnes
Nathan Reed
Neal Dalton
Nessalantha
Nicholas McIntyre
Nicholas Pilon
Nicholas Sokeland
Nick Proud
Nick Townsend
No Reward
Olav Müller
Oliver Scholes
Olivier Nisole
Owen Duffy
Owen Thompson
Pablo Palacios
paolo castelli
Paolo Cecchetto
Patrice Hédé
Patrice Mermoud
Paul Arezina
Paul Baldowski
Paul Olson
Paul Stefko
Paul Tayloe
Paul Yurgin
Pavel Panchekha
Pete
Pete Figtree
Peter Griffith
Peter Kahle
Peter Woodworth
Phil Groff
Philip Harboe Larsen
Philippe Marichal
Philippe Saner
Phillip Webb
Piers Beckley
Porter Williams
R R Clark
R. Brian Scott
Rachael Hixon

Ralf Wagner
Randall Orndorff
Raun Sedlock
Raymond Toghill
Ricardo Gesuatto
Richard Lock
Richard Warren
Rishi Agrawal
Rob Voss
Robert Biskin
Robert Daines
Robert Huss
Robert Rees
Robert Rydlo
Robert Zasso
Rodrigo
Roger Carbol
Roland
Ron Müller
RoninKelt
Roy
Roy LaValley
Ryan Burpee
Ryan D. Kruse
Ryan Good
Ryan Lee
Ryan Macklin
Ryan Olson
Samuel Steinbock-Pratt
Samwise Crider
Sarah Williams
Schubacca
Scot Ryder
Scott Acker
Scott Dexter
Scott Greenleaf
Scott Krok
Scott Martin
Scott Puckett
Scott Thede
Scott Underwood
Scott Wachter
Seán Harnett
Sean M. Dunstan
Sean Nittner
Sean Smith
Sean Smith
Sebastian S
Sergio Le Roux
Seth Clayton
Seth Hartley
Shai Laric
Simon Browne
Simon Brunning
Simon White
Simon Withers
Sion Rodriguez y Gibson
Slawomir Wrzesień
Sophie Lagace
Stefan Feltmann
Stefan Livingstone Shirley
Stefan Schloesser
Stephan A. Terre
Stephanie Bryant

Stephen Caffrey
Stephen Holder
Stephen Hood
Stephen Morring
Stephen Waugh
Steve Ela
Steve Gilman
Steve Kunec
Steve Radabaugh
Steven Code
Steven D Warble
Steven desJardins
Steven K. Watkins
Steven Markley
Steven sims
Steven Whitelock
Svend Andersen
Tabletop Audio
Teresa Oswald
Tevel Drinkwater
The Game's the Thing
The Roach
Thom Terrific
Thomas
Thomas Balls-Thies
Thomas Erskine
Thomas Maund
Tim
Tim
Tim Popelier
Timo
Timothy Seiger
Todd Estabrook
Todd Grotenhuis
Torolf de Merriba
Trevor Crosse
Trevor/Mishy Stellar
Tyler Hunt
Tyson Monagle
Udo Femi
Urs Blumentritt
Victor Allen
Vincent Arebalo
Vladimir Filipović
Wayne Peacock
Wes Fournier
Whitt
William Carroll
William Chambers
William Johnson
William Keller
Winston Crutchfield
WinterKnight
Xavier
Aubuchon-Mendoza
Yong
Z Esgate
Zeb Walker
Zed Lopez
Zolnir
Zonk PJ Demonio
Sonriente

ARE *YOU* READY TO ROLL?

✦ATE DICE™
DICE FOR YOUR FATE & FUDGE GAMES

AVAILABLE NOW

EHP9003	Core Dice		EHP9010	Valentine Dice
EHP9004	Dresden Files:		EHP9011	Vampire Dice
	Winter Knight Dice		EHP9012	Eldritch Dice
EHP9005	Centurion Dice		EHP9013	Antiquity Dice
EHP9006	Atomic Robo Dice			

Find them today at your favorite retailer
or online at www.evilhat.com/dice